The Bible: A Poetic Journey

Nature Photos and Haiku Poems

by

Dwayne Cole

Contents

Dedication

This book is dedicated to all who love the Bible
and want to see it with fresh new eyes,
uniting science and the humanities in a clear
voice of poetry that brings healing for our violent age.
The end goal of biblical poetry, science, and the humanities is
the same—To express, beauty, truth, goodness, in an
adventurous healing spirit. Welcome to—
The Bible: A Poetic Journey.

Preface

In the beginning—
God said, "Let there be."

Shapes emerge.
Colors swirl, bright galaxies form.
Kaleidoscope turns.

Sun, moon, planets spin.
Ocean, womb of change and process.
Beginning and ending.

In time's womb,
plants and animals emerge.
Kaleidoscope turns.

Humans called forth.
Shining, seeing, experiencing.
Kaleidoscope turns.

Science synthesizes.
Einstein theorizes.
Kaleidoscope turns.

Philosophers,
theologians,
speculate.

Moving from force
to luring persuasion.
Zest for adventure.

Perishing—Yet living forever!

Introduction to Bible

A poetic journey
from myth to reality.
Knowing and unknowing.

My wife, Beth, and I have lived with the Bible all our lives.
We grew up in homes where the Bible was read daily,
and in churches where the Bible was taught and preached.
We both have a B. A. degree, majoring in religion.
We met in a Greek class in our first year in seminary as we were
studying for the Master of Divinity degree, and got married
the next year. After we finished that degree, I went on
to receive the Master of Theology degree and a
Ph. D. in New Testament studies, with an emphasis
in New Testament Greek. Beth became a writer of Bible based
curriculum, editor, and manager of editors at LifeWay Christian
Resources. I became a minister in the local church for fifty years,
and an adjunct professor teaching the Bible in college and seminary
classes.

After we retired, we started helping with the care of our
grandchildren in Anchorage, Alaska. We wanted to share
poetry with them, as a way to nurture openness with the
beauty and wonder of nature. Seeing the sparkle in their eyes
helped us to see with the eyes of a child. The tears of joy
washed away some of life's travel stains that cloud our vision.

The wonder of a child blossomed anew in us, becoming
fertile ground for tender teachings and a poetry of kindness.
Looking back on my life-long journey and relationship with the
Bible, like a child, I have more questions than answers.
I discovered God in the Bible looking at me, questioning me,
and luring me to new adventures, falling in doubt, rising in faith.

Retiring in Alaska, I have spent a lot of time since 2011
contemplating in nature and writing nature poetry. Walking in
the beauty and wonder of nature is like going home. A poet is
nature's way of looking at itself, often in paradoxical mythic ideas,
without the need to resolve them.

To say the Bible contains mythic stories does not mean that the
stories are not true. Myth is more than true. The poet uses myth
wrapped in nature images to create sensation rather than fact.
Poetry is well suited for this purpose, especially haiku.

Haiku began in thirteenth-century Japan as the opening lines of
renga, a long oral poem. The short haiku broke away from renga
in the sixteenth century. Haiku, using, colorful images, focuses on
a brief moment in time when we slow down and see nature scenes
like an alpenglow sunrise or sunset transforming the whole sky.
Haiku has a deep appreciation of nature. The Bible is closely
related to nature—mountains, streams, and clouds play a big role
in the Bible. Thus, haiku is especially suited to speak of the

heart beat of the Bible, nature, and our lives. (See my poetry books, *Clouds of Inspiration* and *Lone Leaf Dancing*).

Haiku often ends with a surprising sense of enlightenment. It is in this aha moment that the song bird sings our heart awake, revealing truths from unknown realms. We see with new eyes and hear with new ears, unknowing all that we have known and moving into new adventures. We may not know where we are going, but we feel a new way has been opened. These poems unite science and the humanities in a spirit of kindness, revealing that Way, that Tao moment.

After reading a haiku, one needs to pause and be still to experience this new seeing and hearing. The next haiku may continue this experience or it may move to a new insight.

The format of haiku is three lines, with the first and third line each having 5 syllables, and the second line having 7 syllables. However, the emphasis is on three lines with an economy of words, not a total of 17 syllables.

In this book, I use Alaska nature photographs I have taken as inspiration for my haiku. Poetry inspired by art has been described as ekphrastic—meaning, to draw descriptive images out of the art. The haiku and the photograph share the same space and often complement each other. but not to explain one another. In some instances the haiku and the photograph have little to do with one another. Each can stand alone. Otherwise it would mean that one has been added because the other is not complete or adequate to stand alone.

Haiga is similar to ekphrastic in that it refers to a style of Japanese painting or drawing typically done by haiku poets, and it is often accompanied by a haiku poem. Like haiku, haiga was based on simple everyday observations of nature. Nature photographs can capture this everyday beauty in intuitive ways.

Haibun is a literary form originating in Japan that starts with prose and ends in a haiku. The prose can be short or long. It is often autobiographical. Since I introduce most of the biblical books with a prose statement, followed by haiku, these could be labeled as haibun.

(All biblical quotes used in this book are from The Contemporary English Version, except where noted otherwise).

A Biblical Haibun

Biblical writers knew how to start and end a book. The first verse of the Bible reads, "In the beginning God created the heavens and the earth." (Genesis 1:1). The last verse of the Bible is a prayer wish, "I pray that Jesus will be kind to all of you." (Revelation 22:21). A one sentence summary of the Bible and God, the Poet of the world, is revealed in these bookend verses—The world moves toward kindness.

> God dreams
> Beauty, Wonder, Goodness—
> Kindness to all.

In my preaching and teaching ministry, I faithfully tried to share the beauty and wonder of the Bible with the major theme of kindness to all. This is not an easy task. Walking through the Bible is an adventure filled with obstacles. I have simplified this process by writing my book, *A Relational Hermeneutic of Kindness*. In fact, all my writing and poetry is seen through this lens of kindness. The church and its leaders have taken the Bible and portrayed God in a king's robe and given the traits of Caesar. We have built walls that exclude. The Bible itself has walls. The Temple was encircled by walls that kept people out. Yet, our poetic journey through the Bible will reveal how the good news is always seeking to be free from prejudice and laws that bind. Within the Bible there is a struggle for an unhindered gospel.

Living with our grandchildren from their birth into young adulthood, revealed that the walls erected by biblical writers and its interpreters are very thin in the child's spirit and inquisitive mind. This spirit guides the writing of this book. I believe in truths not yet revealed, in poems not yet written, and in songs not yet sung. Revelation from God did not end with the closing of the Bible. As the Bible ends, the spirit of John the beloved disciple, becomes the guiding principle for my book, *The Bible: A Poetic Journey*: "I pray that Jesus will be kind to all of you." (See Revelation 22:21).

If it seems conceited to suggest that this book reinterprets the Bible and opens a new way to God, please forgive me. My study of the Bible has revealed that each writer and each book seeks to accomplish this calling, The very titles, the Old Testament and New Testament suggest this journey of ever new insights and revelations. Jesus often said, "You have heard it said by men of old, an eye for an eye, a tooth for a tooth; but I say unto you: Love your enemies." Jesus placed a child in his lap and said, "If you want to enter this new time of God, you must become as a little child. In the spirit of a child these poems will sing for you the Bible as you have never heard it. While writing the book, I often woke from dreams, holding my breath, in silence seeing poetic truths unfold.

My poetic journey with the Bible reveals that God is the Supreme Poet inspiring these poetic writings like the Psalms sung in worship settings. Jesus, as the Word incarnate, spoke in poetry. This is not often recognized since Jesus' teachings did not use rhyme, but he did use rhythm; and rhythm is more basic to poetry.

This use of rhythm can be seen in Luke 6:31—

> Treat others
> Just as you want
> to be treated

Matthew 7:7 is a good example of parallel rhythm—

> Ask and you will receive.
> Search and you will find.
> Knock and the door will be opened.

So, when we interpret the Bible as a poetic journey, we are in good company. To be sure, the gospel writers and the church communities redacted these teachings; but there is sufficient evidence to show that Jesus used poetry to help his followers see, hear, remember, and share his gentle Galilean glories. Jesus cared for the outcast. During my ministry I sought to be an ally of LGBTQ+ individuals. This book continues that support. (See my book, Gentle Galilean Glories: The Tender Teachings of Jesus).

Old Testament

"I live my life in ever widening circles,
each superseding all the previous ones.
Perhaps I never shall succeed in reaching
the final circle, but attempt I will.

I circle around God, the ancient tower,
and have been circling for a thousand years,
and still I do not know: am I a falcon,
a storm or a continuing great song?"
—Rainer Maria Rilke

The Bible is a great song of faith stories that circle around God, who is in the world and for the world, in us and for us. I invite you to join me in this adventurous journey of ever widening circles of faith. As members of God's family the world is wider than we can see, and we are a part of that grand vision. We are one in this family. The central song in the Old Testament portion of the Bible is the Exodus from bondage, and the **journey** to the Promise Land. In this journey God covenants to be faithful and show tender care at all times.

This vision of kindness directs our eyes inward and heavenward, mapping our spiritual journey. Are we justified in using kindness as the lens for interpreting God, the Bible, and the world?

Poieo, Poiesis, Poiema, Poietes

In the Septuagint version of the Old Testament (LXX),
this cluster of Greek words with the root meaning
of "to do" or "to make," occurs 3,200 times. They are used
to refer to God miraculously calling creative activity out of chaos,
issuing in colorful light and beauty, a Garden of Eden,
as told in the story of Genesis. They also are used to speak
of God calling forth Adam and Eve, and the people of God,
including you and me.

The same Greek cluster of words are used in the New Testament
568 times to describe God's creative luring activity
as a saving and helping activity seen especially
in the tender teachings of Jesus. This usage is best seen
in Ephesians 2:10, "God planned for us to do good things,
and to live as God has always wanted us to live." That is why
God sent Christ to make us what we are, poiema, "God's
masterpiece." The word, poet, means maker—God is Poet.

In a special sense, poesis, is the word for what is done
by God's artisanship as the poet of the world tenderly saving
all that can be saved. The Epistle of James in the New Testament
calls us to be "doers of the word," as artisans of God's word
modeled in Jesus' tender teachings, The followers of Jesus
are called to be poets of the world doing good works.

In the New Testament this covenant is fulfilled in the gentle life and tender teachings of Jesus—The new exodus of the cross and resurrection is an eternal heart song singing our soul awake to beauty, goodness, and wonder. (See, my books, Gentle Galilean Glories: The Tender Teachings of Jesus; and, A Relational Hermeneutic of Kindness, for a fuller treatment of the question— Are we justified in using kindness as the lens for interpreting the Bible? Also see Appendices A and B at the end of this book for key biblical verses on kindness and words for kindness in the teachings of Jesus). A poetry of kindness is well suited to speak about the Bible, God, and the world. Poetry can express the depth of mystical truths—

Spoken and unspoken, known and unknown.
Poetry is the vehicle of wonder,
using metaphors and images that see
with many eyes and feel with many emotions,
moving beyond the temporal to sing eternal truths.
One of the most cherished chapters in the Bible
is First Corinthians 13, known as the love chapter.
Verse 4 is the heartbeat of this love poem—"Love is patient;
love is kind; love is not envious or boastful or arrogant."
Almost every translation equates love and kindness.

I was born into a family of kindness.
In the words and actions of my parents
kindness was hidden and revealed.

Kindness is reciprocal
and heals both the ones giving
and the ones receiving.

Genesis

The name, Genesis, originates from a Greek word
that means beginning. The first part of the Book of Genesis
is about the beginning of all things, with special emphasis
on the beginning of the people of Israel. Someone asked
a Jewish Rabbi why God favored Israel. He responded,
God calls all people. Israel heard and responded to the call
that lures everyone toward beauty and love.
The writers of Genesis were guided by this principle—

Out of darkness and chaos,
the world moves toward
light and goodness.

Genesis tells the mythic story of Adam and Eve,
as representative of all people, and how human disobedience
brought sin into the world that spread rapidly. The majority of
the book of Genesis tells the faith story of Abraham and Sarah
and how God promised to bless their descendants,
with the promise—"God will take care of you and lead you on
your journey to the Land of Promise (Based on Genesis 50:24).

God dreamed
The light that we cannot see
Shines for everyone

Poet of the world

Painting sunrise art scenes

First day of creation

On first day God said

I command light to shine

Called the light day

God separated

Light from darkness

Called darkness night

God rested and said

It is all good, very good

Humans are the rest of God

Genesis, the first book of the Bible, starts with a creation myth. Even children know that the Genesis account in the opening pages of the Bible is not actual history. Our grandson at the age of ten came home from school and said, the Bible story of creation can't be true. It says that God created the world in 6 days and rested on the 7th day.

I sat down and listened to my grandson. In the first decade of
his life he had already lived in an "ever widening circle." He had
traveled to many parts of the world on vacation with his parents.
He had a sense of how vast the world and the universe were.
His teacher had read the creation story in Genesis as a literal
story of how the world began. She did not talk about our
understanding of science, evolution, and myth. She read the
Bible story as an historical account of creation. I spent an hour just
listening and sharing a few important things about myth.
Without giving a detailed account of our talk, I will let these two
haiku express our conversation.

Sitting like sibyls
Gathering our lives
Crystal ball gazing

Mythic reality
woven as one faith story
of kindness and love

Exodus

No experience had a greater impact on ancient Israel than the exodus from Egypt. So central was this event to Israel's self-understanding that it formed the basis of Israel's covenant with God at Mount Sinai. When giving Moses the Ten Commandments, God begins by explaining, "I am the Lord your God, who brought you out of Egypt ... You shall have no other gods before me" (Exodus 20:2–3). The exodus experience also provided the moral impetus behind many of Israel's laws. From the Exodus experience, the people of God learned about the proper treatment of foreigners. Leviticus 19:34 commands: "You shall treat the stranger who lives with you as a fellow citizen. You shall love the stranger as you love yourself, for you were once strangers in the land of Egypt." And regarding those most vulnerable in society, Deuteronomy 24:17–18 instructs: "Do not withhold justice from an outsider or an orphan, and do not take the cloak of a widow in pledge. Remember that you were slaves in Egypt and that the Lord your God redeemed you from there. Therefore, I am commanding you to do this."

My photo of Denali reminds me of Moses at Sinai

Out of Egypt
Free from slavery
God hears our pleas

Mount Sinai laws
I am your God, follow me
The ten commandments

Denali sits beyond the tundra
Ruling upon her throne
The Great One is everywhere

Inviting all to come
and gaze upon beauty
Play around jeweled breasts

Climb to highest peak
Sit quietly contemplating
See with new eyes

See where earth ends
and heaven begins
Cherubim sing alleluia

Leviticus

Leviticus was also shaped by the experience of the exodus from Egypt. The exodus experience provided the moral impetus behind many of Israel's laws concerning the proper treatment of foreigners. The central theme of Leviticus can be seen in chapter 19:33-34, expressed here in haiku verse—

> Remember,
> you were once foreigners
> in the land of Egypt.

> Don't mistreat foreigners
> who live in your land. Instead,
> love them as yourself.

Compassion for foreigners did not always include accepting members of their own community. Leviticus is clearly prejudiced toward women and slaves, and it has been used by many conservative church groups to forbid ordination of women to ministry and seeing same sex relationships as sinful (See 18:22). The Old Testament teachings of kindness and the gentle teachings of Jesus in the New Testament leave these prejudicial laws behind.

Numbers

The book of Numbers recounts the history of God's people after they escape from Egyptian bondage. The multitudes were discouraged and found it difficult to believe that God was with them and cared for them. Aaron's prayer in Numbers 6:24-26, using Moses' teachings, offers hope. This inspiring prayer gives encouragement to God's people in all ages.—

I pray that God

will bless and protect us

with loving kindness.

God is good to us.

Our shield and defender

gives us peace and joy.

Deuteronomy

The book of Deuteronomy is about the patient love of God.
When God's people forget, Moses gives the instructions
from God a second time—Love God with all your heart, soul,
and strength. Memorize this and teach it to your children over
and over again. This commandment nurtured Jesus' tender teachings
and became the Great Commandment.

Moses rescued you

from bondage in Egypt land,

cared for you in wanderings.

First commandment is—

Love God with your whole heart.

Love all God's people.

Joshua

The book of Joshua also tells the story of God's patient luring
leadership. The mantle is passed from Moses to Joshua.
The promised land, Canaan, was not all sweetness and light.
It was a challenging and fearful time. Joshua's faith broke down
barriers and walls.

Times up.

Put your pencils down.

The test is over.

What about our feelings?
What about our anxieties?
Can we put them down?

Joshua said,

sun stand still, and clock stopped.

Moon and stars still shine.

Pencil up, write love.

The times of our feelings

not the same as clock.

Choose to worship God;

and obey God faithfully,

as my family does.

Judges

My life was never the same after encountering the tooth rattling dissonance of the Judges. The book of Judges is a call to be strong. The journey story continues the history of Israel after Joshua's death. God raised up a series of tribal leaders, called Judges. Empowered by God, the Judges delivered the people of Israel from their enemies. In the Book of Judges we see God nurturing a covenant people who will give to the world great prophets, and Jesus as a worthy model for all humans.

The stories of the Judges are about intellectual and spiritual daring. In these stories we learn that God calls people to be strong and bold, overcoming doubt and human weakness. This was especially true of Deborah's story told in Judges, chapter 4 in prose and in chapter 5 in poetry or psalm format. In chapter 4 we learn that Deborah was a prophet and judge in Israel during a violent time when the people of God faced extinction from warfare. While Deborah was the only female judge, she was the first; and she set a judicial precedence for the twelve judges who came after her. Deborah was noted for her civil and social contributions. In Deborah we see God present with Israel in her time of great need, and this is the main lesson we should learn from this story.

Deborah helped me to learn that God lures creation with loving aims and purposes and spreads a banquet table before us. Then God invites us to the party. Here is the image that shapes my view of God in these biblical stories:

Deborah arose

A mother in Israel

To save her people

This wisdom seed of seeing God like the tender care of a mother is planted in Deborah's song, it grows in the Psalms of Israel: "I have learned to feel safe and satisfied, just like a child on its mother's lap. People of Israel, you must trust the Lord now and forever" (Psalm 131), and comes to fruition in Jesus' tender teachings.

Deborah took command

God was kind to Israel

Mother protects child

Feel satisfied

Like child on it's mother's lap

Trust God forever

God is purposeful

God is loving

God is personable

Ruth

The book of Ruth shows one Israelite family, featuring Ruth and her mother-in-law, Naomi, during the time of the Judges. The story is an important link in Old Testament history, for one of Ruth's great grandchildren was King David. The spirit of this Old Testament book is expressed in Ruth's dedication found in 1:16-17—

I will go where you go.

I will live where you live;

your people will be my people.

your God will be my God.

I will die where you die

and be buried beside you.

1 and 2 Samuel

First and second Samuel are two parts of one book about Samuel, the last judge to lead Israel before the time of kings, Saul and David. Samuel illuminates this transition.

Sparkle in his eyes.
David comes before Samuel—
"He is the one!"

Spirit of the Lord
Came to David with power
Anointed with oil

These two Old Testament books, like a modern novel, are filled with insurrections, battles of war, betrayal, rape, murders, and despair. Perhaps the value of these books is to show how violence reaps violence. Most of these two books is best left behind.

1 and 2 Kings

Like First and Second Samuel, First and Second Kings are two parts of one book. They were divided because they were too large to fit on one scroll. In addition to recounting the life of the kings, these books include the story of Elijah, one of Israel's greatest prophets.

When seeking a vision, one must be able to see beyond that which is concrete; and see through the lens of God's kindness! There is a great need for a fresh vision, especially with youth. Many are seeking spiritual guidance, while having little interest in organized religion.

1 Kings 19:1-15, is an example of how God comes to sit beside tired and weary Elijah and all seeking to do God's work; and whispers, "Don't quit. You are not alone." Then reaching tender arms around him says, "Together we will transform the broken patterns into a masterwork of creative art."

Wishing to encourage her son's progress on the piano, a mother took him to a Paderewski concert. After they were seated, the mother spotted a friend in the audience and walked down the aisle to greet her. When the house lights dimmed, the mother returned to her seat and saw that her son was missing. Suddenly, the curtains parted. and spotlights focused on the grand piano on stage. In horror, the mother saw her little boy sitting at the keyboard, pecking out "Twinkle,

Twinkle, Little Star." Paderewski made his entrance, moved to the piano, whispering, "Keep playing." Paderewski reached down and began to fill in a bass part. Soon he reached around the child and added a running obligato. Together the master and young novice transformed a frightening situation into a wonderfully creative experience. And the audience was mesmerized.

If you are weary in seeking to do good, God comes to you and whispers, "Don't quit. You are not alone." Then reaching tender arms around you says, "Together we will transform the broken patterns into a masterwork of creative art."

Moonless Midnight and Dawn of New Day

Alaska morning
Dark as a moonless midnight
Light hides in darkness

The national news
All about killing and war
I've heard this before

When will we learn
Killing begets more killing—
Vengeance reaps vengeance.

War that ends all wars
Will be a nuclear war
This is our only world

Travelled to the moon
It is not for humans
No man in the moon

Have rovers on Mars
It is a long shot by far
Best get along here

1 and 2 Chronicles

Like First and Second Samuel and First and Second Kings, First
and Second Chronicles are two parts of one book. They
were also divided because they were too large to fit on one
scroll. The books of Chronicles have gotten lost as though they
were a pale shadow of the previous Writings. They are not
included in the common lectionary, so those sitting in the pew of
churches do not hear the courageous and practical message of
the Chronicles. That main message is this: The living God is
present and working in the faith community. Trust God's
wondrous transforming energy that is seeking justice
everywhere on earth. (See I Chronicles 16:11-18)

Praise God forever

Glory seen everywhere

God sees our needs

Ezra

King Cyrus of Persia allowed the people of God to return to their land and rebuild the temple. Ezra's prayer in chapter 9:8-9 challenged them to be faithful and worship God.

Weeping shall cease.
People of God shout for joy!
God is good to us.

Praise God, my people!
God treats us with kindness.
God helps us.

God loves us.
Gives us new life.
Shows great kindness.

Nehemiah

Nehemiah, a personal servant of king Artaxerxes, was allowed to rebuild the walls of Jerusalem. When they were completed, the people of God saw this as a sign that God was blessing them.

Nehemiah promised them that God was merciful and faithful in keeping promises. He challenged them in 8:17 to celebrate with great joy and to be faithful, loving God and one another—

Nehemiah
prophesied about good times
Glory of God near

Lead by a star
The wise will follow
Find new joy

The Book of Nehemiah closes in chapter 13:22 with the encouraging prayer—

God is merciful
Pray for God's kindness to come
Bless all people

Esther

The book of Esther tells how Esther became the new queen of King Xerxes. She was advised not to publicize her Jewishness. So the name of God does not appear in Esther. She was brave and saved her people.

Woman named Esther
Named queen by King Xerxes
Esther saved Israel

Esther risked her life
to save Israel, her people.
Born to be a Savior!

Job

The book of Job is about searching for the meaning of
deep suffering, and whether God is with us in our suffering.
Job's friends could not help him. Job found that only God
had the wisdom that gives help in facing life's challenges.

In troubling times, Job becomes relevant. Using wisdom imagery
expressed in poetry, especially haiku, can give us new insights. In the
three simple lines of haiku, aha moments are seen; and in these times
God is present to help us.

I took the photo above that magically shows a Leviathan leaping
from the water, in Hawaii at sunrise, 2018. It is unaltered, except for
one small dot—I added the eye. I added the haiku poems using
apocalyptic images from Isaiah, Job, Amos, Psalms, and Revelation.
The photo and other poems are on pages 70-71, of my book,
Poet of the Universe: A Vision of Beauty and Goodness.

Great leviathan
leaps from the sea with open mouth
in pursuit of fish.

Jaws with sharp teeth.
Monster sneezes, lightning flashes.
Smoke billows from nose.

Sparks and flames explode.
Eyes glowing as coals of fire.
Blazing breath singes!

The fiery monster—
All cringe in fear as he leaps.
Hell licks its chops!

Job did not find satisfactory answers to his suffering, but he learned
to live the questions. Job 19:25-27 expresses the faith that one day
he would live into the answers—

My Savior lives

My flesh may be destroyed

One day I'll see God

Once dark clouds disperse

Job learned that God was fair

Shines greater than sun

God abundantly

blesses Job with a long life

He finds happiness

(See Job 42:10-17)

(I could not leave Job without sharing his mythic story of the unicorn on the next three pages. This story invites us all to go forward holding our head high with new-found strength.)

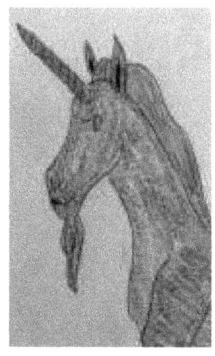

Unicorn Anyone?

In Jewish folklore

the legendary unicorn was so monstrous

that Noah had to strap the pair

to his ark with the nostrils

inside the ark so they could breathe.

The King James

translators of the Bible,

knowing of this mysterious myth,

brought this long vanished

creature of legend into

their circle of faith

by rendering the Hebrew word

for wild ox, as unicorn,

in several Old Testament readings.

The most notable reference

to the unicorn is found in Job 39:9-12.,

"Will the unicorn be willing to serve thee,

or abide by thy crib?

Canst thou bind the unicorn

with band in the furrow?

Will he harrow the valleys after thee?

Wilt thou trust him,

because his strength is great?

Wilt thou leave thy labour to him?

Wilt thou believe him,

that he will bring home thy seed,

and gather it into thy barn?"

Part 2

Siting in silent contemplation

on Job's account of the unicorn,

with the last rays of the setting sun dancing

I waited.

With the patience of Job,

I waited.

Till the moon rose in the night sky.

I waited.

Then the unbelievable happened!
The legendary unicorn stood before me
with white body taking on a blue/purple hue
Reflecting the moonlight.
His one unique magic horn
rising on his forehead---
Proudly held high
as a symbol of strength
like the spire of Solomon's temple.
Unicorns are for real!
At least in Mythic poetry!
Where they will live forever!
Inviting us all to go forward
holding our head high
in new found strength
With the mystery of the universe
In the eyes of this ancient mythic legend
shining in us!

"You are my mighty rock, my fortress, my protector, the rock where I am safe, my place of shelter" (Psalm 18:2).

Photo taken in Maine of our son,

Dr. Kevin Dwayne Cole and wife, Susan

Psalms, the longest book in the Bible, has 150 poems that sing the major themes of the Bible—thanksgiving, praise, sorrow, and hope. They continue to hold a special place in the hearts of the people of God. The 23rd Psalm is perhaps the best known and loved. It inspired my poem—

Seeing wild flowers,
I know God is my shepherd.
God is good.

On dark Alaska nights,
God is caring for me.
I am not afraid.

Grace fills my cup
until it is overflowing.
I experience peace.

Each day of my life,
kindness is with me.
I will live for God.

I rise early

to meditate on the mystery of time—

To feel sunrise on my face.

Experience

time wrapped in eternity—

God is eternal.

Eternal now

in these fleeting moments—

Destiny and hope.

In contemplation,

eternity is present—

With us now.

As the sun rises,

darkness is overcome.

Eternal light shines!

Let your Kindness shine brightly on us.
(Psalm 3:6)

D. Cole

A Key Verse for Living the Psalms

"Calm down and learn that I am God." —Psalm 46:10

The quieter you become, the more you are able to hear.—Rumi

The quieter you are
The more you can see and hear
Be still and know God
Solitude in the beauty of nature
Nurtures calmness of our soul

(This is also a key verse for Understanding The Bible: A Poetic Journey).

Proverbs

Kindness to the poor shows
respect to God the creator
(See Proverbs 14:31)

Like Psalms, the book of Proverbs is pure poetry. It is best seen as short powerful wisdom statements in the spirit of Solomon, yet attributed to God. The simplicity of these short poetic statements make them easy to memorize and apply to daily living, especially to the needs of the poor.

Wisdom is God's gift
for living right every day
at home and in community

Life's adventure
God's dream for the world of humans
Kindness to the poor

Trust in God
Wear love as a necklace
Live mindfully

Ecclesiastes

There is a voice that doesn't use words. Listen. —Rumi

Ecclesiastes has often been seen as a gloomy outlook on life. Yet, it can best be seen as a search in ordinary life for extraordinary meaning and purpose. What is meaning of God relating to humans in all ages and ages to come? God's covenantal relationship to Israel, God incarnate in Jesus, is the biography of God.

Respect for God's ways.
This is what life is about—
Sing Alleluia!

I walk in nature
See Sol rushing across sky
Painting the clouds

A snowshoe hare squalls
All of Nature is weeping
Lynx with food for kits

Searching for meaning
Stained with bloodshed and travail
Grief of centuries falls

Pain of families
Fleeing from persecution
Sadness rings in ears

Look up at the sky
Blazing in glory for all
God's light shines

Search for meaning in life
We crave beauty and goodness
Yet haunted by loss

Who told the geese
It was time to take wing and fly
Opening magic vistas

Song of Songs

The title, Song of Songs, means "the most beautiful of songs." It is sometimes called the Song of Solomon. It could be taken as a book of poems about powerful love between two persons.

The passion of love,

more powerful than death—

Bursting into flame.

Rose of Sharon,

Lily of the valley—

Awake to Love.

Kiss me tenderly!

Your love is better than wine.

You smell so sweet.

You are my garden.

Hurry to me, my darling!

Sweetness of spice.

Isaiah

The theme of the Book of Isaiah is expressed most clearly in 65:17-25, as a new creation—forgetting the past, and creating a new heaven and a new earth. Thus, it is a call for celebration in a new Jerusalem where there will be no more crying or sorrow.

Those who trust the Lord will find new strength.

They will be strong like eagles
soaring upward on wings;
without getting tired. (Isaiah 40:31).

Does the eagle kiss
the rainbow as it flies on high?
Joy of new sunrise!

Soar on eagles' wings.
Live eternity's sunrise.
Be strong!

Mother's love for child
Model of God's love for Israel
an unfailing love

Monster storms pounding.
Nature caught on rampage.
Without angel wings!

Zip your raincoat good.
God's people bend into the wind.
Rainbow appears!

Jeremiah

I brought you into a fertile land to eat its fruit and rich produce.

But you came and defiled. —Jeremiah 2:7

I will be kind.
I will bless you with a future
filled with hope.
—Jeremiah 29:10-11

God desires beauty

Calls us to be co-laborers

Nurture the world

Be kind to nature

Care for streams, rivers, oceans

Responsible gardeners

Climate change is real

Wake up and move the world

Beauty blossoms

Heart Ache (Jeremiah 9:24)

When the world becomes fearful
and my heart aches with pain,
I walk among the flowers,
while the dew is still on the roses.

Beauty waits beyond fear—
The light of love is blazing.
When I walk in the garden,
I feel and see love overcoming fear.

In the garden the flowers
and the birds sing to me saying,
I am loved and held in goodness.
The music calls me to go—

Share love with
all of God's children.
Show justice and mercy
to everyone on earth.

Sit in the garden

Full of gleaming beauties

Adventure awaits

Secrets to reveal

Baton magically lifted

Butterflies softly singing

Elves dancing

Bees humming a soft tune

Spirits rise

Gnomes dreaming

Garden singing poems

Sit quietly

What God liked best is showing kindness, Justice, and mercy to everyone on earth. (Jeremiah 9:24).

What God likes best
is showing kindness,
justice, and mercy to all.

—Jeremiah 9:24

I am everywhere—
both near and far,
in heaven and on earth.
—Jeremiah 23:23-24

To say that God is
in the world and for the world
In us and for us has ramifications
for the way we treat the world
and the way we treat each other.

Artificial lines drawn
between race and gender
are artificial.

Lamentations

Lamentations is a book of five lament poems expressing deep sorrow about the destruction of Jerusalem. Like the lament Psalms, the poems move toward hope. When you turn back God will be merciful. This major theme can be see in Lamentations 3:21-24, expressed in these three haiku.

Remembering

fills me with a living hope.

God's kindness never fails!

God is merciful.

Keeps from destruction.

God can be trusted.

Mercy each morning.

Assurance deep in my heart.

Can depend on God.

Ezekiel

"Can these bones come back to life?"

—Ezekiel 37:1-14

Magic lies in poetry that speaks the seemingly impossible.

Nature has been revealing mysterious possibilities from the

beginning of time. Truths hidden in the dead bones

buried in a prophetic biblical story are danced into life again

by the rhythm of Ezekiel's poetry.

Magically,
the wind of the Spirit blew.
Flowers freshened up.

Dead bones arise,
wrapped in muscle and skin.
Breathe life again!

D. Cole

Ezekiel's Rainbow of Hope

I have great faith

in kindness

Brought by rainbows

Faith in deep yearnings
of the soul
not yet fulfilled

See rainbows
Slow down
Take off shoes

Listen
Remember
Forgive

Breathe deep
Recover from fears
Heal

Hope
Wrapped
in goodness

Part II

We gazed into a beautiful rainbow.
Felt we were not of this time and place.
Gazed and waited.

Then Nature's Beauty looked back at us.
We became one with the visible universe.
Security, Promise, and Hope within us.

Ascended into higher realms unknown.
Awakened by Beauty and Grace.
Emboldened by nature's tender touch.

Began to see with new eyes—
All our fears and pains were drawn
into the heart of Kindness.

Overcome with Goodness.
The strength of Oneness in us.
Unbounded Joy!

Joy of being
kissed by a Lover—
Dancing in a new day.

Finding
one's name written
in the shining clouds.

The gift
is buried treasure—
Hope, Beauty, Wonder!

(I used this photo and address
some of these thoughts in my book,
God and Evil: An Ode to Kindness.)

Daniel

Daniel was taken as a prisoner to Babylon.

He rose to a position of power,

but remained faithful to the God of Israel.

The Book of Daniel reports visions Daniel had,

and these visions were interpreted by angels.

I saw what looked like

a son of man

coming with the clouds of heaven,

and he was presented

to the Eternal God.

He was crowned king,

and given power and glory,

so that all people of every

nation and race

would serve him.

He who rules forever,

and his kingdom is eternal,

never to be destroyed. (Daniel 7:13-14).

Daniel in the Lion's Den

The God of Daniel
The living God of Glory
Rescues people

God is faithful
Worship and honor God
Reigns forever

Hosea

"Your goodness is as the morning cloud,
and as the early dew it goes away."
—Hosea 6:4

Hosea was prophet in the northern kingdom of Israel
during its final days as a nation. Hosea's marriage to Gomer
and his family life becomes a picture of the message
he felt called by God to preach to Israel. This picture of rejection
and renewal is seen in 14:4-7—

You've rejected me.
My anger has gone away.
I will heal you.

You will blossom like lilies
and have roots like a tree—
Branches of beauty.

Once Israel returns to God, Hosea in 2:19-20,
promises that they will experience peace and learn justice.

You will live in peace.
Justice, fairness, love, and kindness
is my name.

Hosea described God in chapter 11
as a Mother caring for her child.

Hosea was a big influence on Jesus' tender teachings.

I love you as a child
I feed you at my breast
I taught you to walk

In Hosea's imagery,
God is transitioning—
From male to female.

Joel

"I am merciful, kind, and caring." (Joel 2:13).

Joel expresses the character of ministry

as a kind and caring spirit modeled on God's kindness.

God is a fortress

A safe place for the faithful

God is merciful

Kindness Blessing

May kindness be in our thoughts,

making them good and loving.

May kindness be in our eyes,

leading us to see what is just in life.

May kindness be in our hands and feet

so that we may be of service to others.

May kindness be in our whole being –

Making us one with God, one with all people, and

one with the universe.

(This kindness prayer

was published in my book,

A Relational Hermeneutic of Kindness.

This book will also help you see the importance

of interpreting the Bible and all of life

through the lens of God's merciful and kind Spirit).

Amos

Amos was a sheep herder, not a professional prophet.

Amos felt called of God to deliver this message found in 6:15—

Choose good over evil
See that justice is done to all
God will be kind to you

Amos calls for repentance with the promise of a bright future in 9:7-15. God is presented as a nurturing gardener—

People of God
Repent and you will be saved
Ripen like fruit

You will prosper
Become a fruitful vineyard
Wine will flow freely

Obadiah

Obadiah is so short that it is not divided into chapters.

Obadiah, means worshiper of God. The book is best seen as a call to repent of violent ways and seek God's goodness.

Eagles soar high
They are brought down from the stars
The strong become weak

Vengeance destroys
Feeds on its own anger
Goodness grows strong

Jonah

When most people think about Jonah, they only think of Jonah being swallowed by the whale. However, Jonah presents a kind and merciful picture of God.

God is merciful
Patiently showing kindness
Always showing love
(Jonah 4:2)

My Vision of Jonah

I lie on the snowy mountainside.
Contemplate until I am inside the cloud
shaped like Jonah's whale.

Like Jonah, I reach
for mercy and kindness as a child.
I was filled with joy.

Dark questions arise.
Injustice is seen all around.
The law of the land.

With Jonah let me learn:
"You are a merciful God,
and you are patient.

You always show love,
and you don't like to punish anyone,
not even foreigners" (Jonah 4:2).

Return from the cloud,
a little more tender.
More loving.

Seeking
to show kindness
to all living things.

Micah

Micah 4:3,4 and 6:8 capture the theme of this prophet:

Pound your swords and spears
into rakes and shovels for growing fruit
Live in peace

God told us what's right
See that justice is done
Mercy comes first

D. Cole

Micah uses exodus imagery when God led Israel
with a cloud by day and a fire by night to challenge
the people of God.

Flying Saucer Clouds

Glory forming crystals
Swirling dervish
of creative colors

Cloud dancers
gathering intermingling sunlight
Yellow gold, purple delight

Birth of universe
Spinning into existence
Streaming across sky

Dust particle mystery
Soul arrayed in wonder
Eyes lifted to heaven

Grand adventure
a flying saucer cloud
Galaxy of wonder

Flying to realms unknown—
The realm of celestial
Seraphim.

Nahum

Nahum was a prophet who observed nature. The storms
and whirlwinds were seen as powerful instruments in God's
hands. Yet, he does believe, as seen in 1:7, that God will
patiently lead and lure Israel toward salvation.

Locust are swarming
Devouring your crops
Become caretakers

Your people are sheep
Who have no shepherd to lead
You have no hope

God is good
Protects those in trouble
Trust God forever

Habakkuk

Habakkuk is an ever widening vision of God's glory
that finds its fulfillment in tender teachings.
"I will stand upon my watch tower of prayer." Habakkuk 2:1

Habakkuk's prayer tower
Not built by human hands
Reached into heaven

God's grace and mercy
are its windows and doors.
Open wide and sing!

Aurora Borealis' Glamor Dance

Dervish of colors
Intermingling lights
Green, purple, and blue

Wending giant ribbons
Glory flashing across night sky
Leaping, spinning

From heaven to earth
Swept into Mystery
Soul arrayed in wonder

Eyes lifted to glory!

In this dance
one is swept into the music
of stellar cyclones

Aurora glamor dance

Realm of celestial seraphim

Singing,

Holy!

      Holy!

            Holy!

      Glory

          in the Highest

            Heavens!

Zephaniah

Zephaniah is best seen as a song of celebration that comes after punishment, humbly repenting, and maintaining faithfulness. This poetic song is expressed best in 3:14-20—

Song of Wonder

Sing, be glad.
Rejoice with all your heart.
Rest in God's love.

United in Love
Care for lame and outcast
I will lead you home

Haggai

The time of Haggai was a difficult one for God's people.
Haggai has a message for the suffering of his age, and for all ages
who simply want to survive the rigorous toils of each day.

Temple still not rebuilt. Haggai's message is summarized in 2:1-9.

Rebuild the temple
Enjoy God's blessings
God will be with you

Brightness of God's glory
Will fill you each new day
You will find God's peace

Zechariah

Zechariah shares visions that challenge faithfulness to God.
His vision is summarized in 9:9. This inspiring message is picked
up and shared by Luke and John in the New Testament
in the coming of the Messiah.

Everyone,
celebrate and shout!
Your king has won a victory.

Messiah is coming.
Humble, riding on donkey.
God is coming.

Everyone shout!
Celebrate with praises.
God is coming.

Malachi

Malachi begins his prophetic message, and ends the Old Testament by reminding the people of God—

Israel, I, the Lord, have loved you. I will send a messenger who will shine like the sun with healing in its rays. You will jump around like calves at play. He will lead children and parents to love each other more. (See especially 1:2 and 4:2-6).

On a spring walk in Alaska, Beth and I witnessed—

A Dance of Joy

From behind a tree
We did joyfully see
Mother moose and calf

Nuzzling and kissing
Prancing around
sharing a laugh

Dancing with each other
Love they did make
Joy they did partake

With foreheads caressing
Passing to each, important
Secret messaging

I'm yours forever,
and you are forever mine.
Family felicity!

Wildflowers were still.
Trees, mountains, skies, and birds
all sharing the thrill.

All seemed to breathe
Audible prayer of wonder
Heaven was open

Beth and I link hands
Join the dance of mystery—
I am yours, you are mine.

For

all

Eternity!

(This dramatic performance
reminded me of Malachi's vision
that closes the Old Testament faith stories.)

The New Testament

I have been inspired by the Celtic concept of "thin places." The New Testament is a thin place where God meets us with a new vision for our lives and for the world. A thin place reminds us that God is present with wonder in every moment of life and in each entity we encounter. In the New Testament, Light shines in Bethlehem at Jesus' birth and from that shining our world is changed forever.

Haiku, in three simple lines, captures this thin place of an ordinary event. Yet shining in this thin place that is created is an ever widening circle of love, and in that loving event God is present.

(For a more complete story of the New Testament see my book, *The Story of the Bible: Authority, Inspiration, Canonization, and Translation*).

Gospel of Matthew

Into our hate filled world, Jesus comes uninvited.
Comes for all who have no room to lay their head.
Jesus is present for all the poor and homeless.

Gospel of Matthew
The Good News of Jesus' birth
Center of our faith

Mary and baby Jesus
The message of kindness and love
Heaven's approval

Light Dispels Darkness

The people who sat in darkness have seen a great light, and for
those who sat in the region and shadow of death light has dawned."
—Matthew 4:16

What about the name, darkness? In the New Testament Gospels,

light, Jesus, and God are One in pushing back the shadow of death.

In the Bible as a whole darkness is uncreated light. Unlike light, darkness does not have energy of its own. It is only as the syllables of darkness become words like fear and hate lodged in our hearts that they become the grammar of our lives and rob our love energies leaving the shadow of death in their wake. The shadow of darkness can not overcome light, but sun/Son light has an energy that can dispel darkness and bring the gift of good news.

Naming the Darkness

Jesus went throughout Galilee, teaching in their synagogues and proclaiming the good news of God's glory and curing every disease and every sickness among the people. Matthew 4:23

A crucial question is "How do we overcome darkness?" Acknowledging and naming the darkness as a shadow within us is a first step. We tend to deny our darkness and name it in others. In Mark 7:14-23 Jesus saw the darkness located in the human heart and named it as evil. After naming the darkness, Jesus sought to take possession of the heart for the good news of the glory of God. So the second and most important thing we can do to overcome our darkness is to give our life to Jesus. Jesus then replaces fear and hate with faith, hope, love, and kindness. Jesus as Light is the power that warms, heals, and energizes life.

Walking With Jesus

As Jesus walked by the Sea of Galilee, he saw two brothers, Simon, who is called Peter, and Andrew his brother. . . he said to them,

"Follow me." Immediately they left their nets and followed Jesus.

Matthew 4:18-20

Walking by the Sea,
Jesus called helpers.
Earth and heaven meet.

In Jesus we see
God as the poet of the world
painting beautiful scenes.

Showing tender care.
Nurturing all in beauty
and goodness.

Jesus takes Peter's hand,
and keeps him from sinking
in the stormy sea.

Faith, the road traveled
between earth and heaven—
Kindness is the Way.

The thrill of sunrise
First dawn of new world
Walking in dawn's light

my soul trembles
with ecstasy's bright light
the road we take to happiness

Taking Jesus' hand
we hear, Peace I instill
Can face life's trials

Jesus, Star Thrower,
reach down and save us.
Give abundant life.

"Jesus went throughout Galilee,
teaching in their synagogues and proclaiming
the good news of God's glory."
—Matthew 4:23

(See my book, *Gentle Galilean Glories: The Tender Teachings of Jesus*, for an explanation of why I translate Kingdom of God as God's glory. I show how glory translates Jesus's message of good news best. Kingdom carries the connotation in our world as dominion and ruling power that is often oppressive).

The Sermon on the Mount

In Matthew 6:25-29, Jesus spoke of the birds of the air
and flowers of the field—

Seeing and hearing birds,
the brain makes melodic music.
My heart is thankful.

Graceful beauties
Dance upon the wind
Making music

Smelling flowers
Soul enraptured
Spirit breathes

Thank you for the grace
of your blossoms
Sweetness of your breast

Sprinkling
Heaven's colors
Along my path

Seeing how God cares

For birds and flowers
I trust God's care

Healing for Our Brokenness

As the disciples followed Jesus, they learned that he was a healer and was calling them to share in his miraculous ministry. As I answered the call of discipleship over 50 years ago, I thought this was the primary purpose of the call to follow Jesus. However, I soon learned that the church has skipped over the first purpose of these healing stories. You and I must first see ourselves as the wounded person along the path of life needing healing ourselves.

As Mathews account of the gentle Galilean ministry of Jesus comes to an end, he has this news bulletin—

Breaking News: Matthew 23:37-39

God has transitioned
Became a mother hen
Gathering her chicks

The ministry of Jesus was filled with acts of compassion revealing that the glory of God was coming near. God who spoke and brought light out of darkness— God spoke in Jesus and brought wholeness out of brokenness and life out of death. It was by the power of these love energies of God that Jesus was able to perform his miracles. Jesus' gentle Galilean glories brought new levels of energy in the broken persons and brought catharsis and wholeness.

The gentle life
and tender teachings of Jesus
spread quickly.

And why not?
Heavenly light was overcoming
the darkness of evil.

(You can find an expansion of these gentle teachings in my book, Gentle Galilean Glories: The Tender Teachings of Jesus).

The Gospel of Mark

Mark was the first Gospel written. Matthew and Luke together use over ninety percent of Mark in their Gospels. Since Mark does not start his Gospel with the birth narratives of Jesus, the canon organizers placed Matthew first, and Mark second. Mark highlights the teachings of Jesus that give instructions for living a life of faith. (See Mitzi Minor, The Spirituality of Mark, for an excellent treatment of this theme).

I was introduced to Saint Francis in seminary 53 years ago. His servant prayer is an excellent guide in living the spiritual life—

> Lord, make me an instrument of thy peace.
> Where there is hatred, let me sow love,
> Where there is injury, pardon;
> Where there is doubt, faith;
> Where there is despair, hope;
>
> Where there is darkness, light;
> And where there is sadness, joy.
> O Divine Master, grant that I may not so much seek
> to be consoled as to console, t
> to be understood as to understand,
> to be loved, as to love.
> For it is in giving that we receive,
> It is in pardoning that we are pardoned,
> and it is in dying that we are born to eternal life.
> —St. Francis of Assisi

Our Times: Our political climate today reveals an alarming moral backwardness and spiritual deterioration. There is a need for a deeper understanding of the psyche of the individual human being. It is easy to escape responsibility by pointing to the shadow in others. It is essential that we focus on our own individual psyche, for it is out of our human heart that all future evil comes (a prominent theme in the writings of C. G. Jung).

Jesus located evil in the human heart (See Mark 7:14-23). Then he sought to take possession of our heart for the glory of God.

The Central Message of Mark

God's glory is near
to meet each event of life
with kindness.

God is kind.
Jesus lived and taught kindness.
Spirit empowers kindness.

Jesus's parables
Pure poetry in rhythm
God dancing with us

God calls all people
to respond in kindness
God is kindness

We cannot give
all the kindness the world needs.
World needs all we can give.

Cross of Jesus
Sacrificial love action
Walking in humility

Jesus, God's flower
Blossomed into heaven
A resurrection

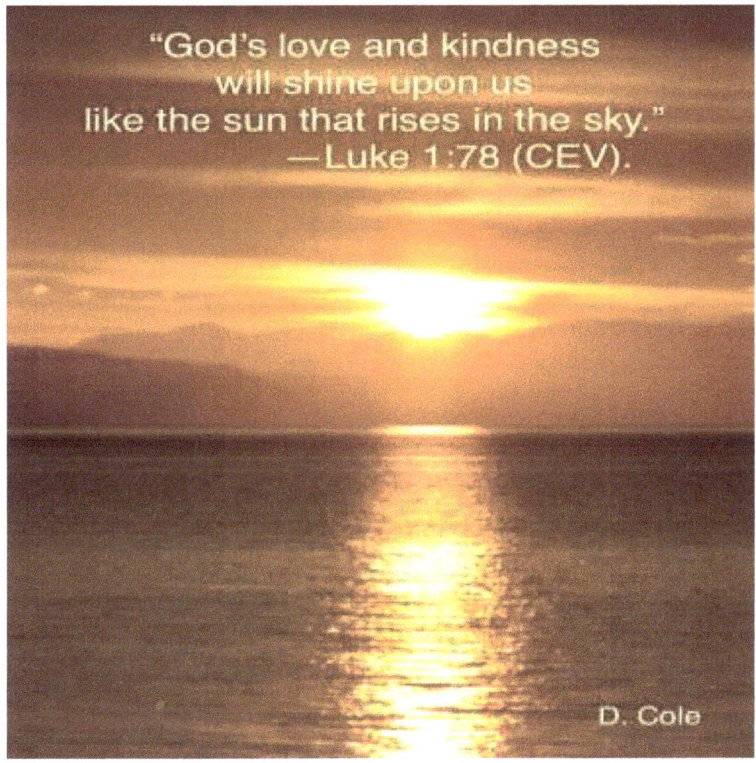

(Photo taken from the spit in Homer, Alaska).

I will be kind
I will bless you with a future
filled with hope.

"God's love and kindness
will shine on us like the sun
that rises in the sky."

—Luke 1:78

These verses invite us to pray for all who are filled
with fear and suffering. May God's goodness and kindness
sustain you, replacing your fear with adventurous faith
and hope seen in each new golden sunrise!

"Love your neighbors as much
as you love yourself." Luke 10:27

Jesus spoke a parable that is relevant for our evil age—

"When an evil spirit leaves a person,
it travels through the desert,
looking for a place to rest.
But when it doesn't find a place,
it says, "I will go back to the home
I left." When it gets there and finds
the house clean and fixed up, it goes
off and finds seven other evil spirits
even worse than itself. They come
and make their home there, and
that person ends up in worse shape
than before. —(Luke 11:24-26).

I shot the devil
and he came back bringing seven more
from his demon pack.

I dropped my bombs
blowing doors of hell, releasing
a legion of demons.

To walk to and fro
on the earth, wreaking havoc.
Nature of vengeance.

Grows with each new act.
I shot the devil, he came back
bringing seven more.

Hell is swallowing
our poor, our homeless, our refugees,
and disadvantaged.

Our pandemic world is upside down.
Walking on my favorite trail in Alaska,
I wear my protective mask.

If I meet a hiker not wearing a mask,
I step off the trail,
and hide behind a tree.
Stay hidden for five minutes,
for the dangerous thief to pass,
and for the air to clear.
The person wanting to be safe,
and for all others to be protected
is wearing the mask that once
marked one as a thief.
The unmasked person
is the thief in our upside down

Pandemic world.
Love your neighbor.
Wear your mask.

The Gospel of John

"In the beginning was the one who is called the Word."
—John 1:1

Oh Mighty Poet
Visionary dreamer of joy
Flashes of glory

Mystery of words
made flesh in tender teachings
that transform and heal

"God so loved the world. . . ." John 3:16

God is in the world
Loving and giving to all
Guidance for living

Mother moose
tenderly nuzzling
newborn calf

Love pantomime
Eternity is in the dance
Loving and giving

We are in
this beautiful world
To give love

Dancing with God
and our world family
Our reason for being

Lenten Gifts

"I am the bread from heaven that gives life!
The one who eats this bread in faith will live forever."

(Paraphrase of John 6:48-50)

Lent, time of stillness
emptying the soul of noise,
filling with goodness.

There is a sweetness
hiding in quietness,
desiring to be shared.

We are the vessels
waiting to be filled with
gifts from heaven.

Jesus pours the wine.
Breaks the bread.
Remember me.

Come to the Lenten table
where all are fed—
Gifts of life.

mystery of flesh words
light that transforms and heals
God so loves the world

Jesus' miracles
Signs of divine healing love
Giving gift of life

Jesus is the Way
The eternal truth
and everlasting life

Acts

We sing forever
Jesus is ascended
Joy and peace our gifts
—Acts 1:8-9

Acts is a sequel to the Gospel of Luke, both written by the
same author. Acts can best be described as the struggle
for an unhindered spreading of the good news of the
gospel as it moves into the non-Jewish world of the Gentiles—
"Tell everyone about me in Jerusalem and all Judea, in Samaria,
and everywhere in the world." (Acts 1:8).
Luke gives in Acts a detailed account of Paul's missionary
journeys, Paul bravely preached the glory of God from Jerusalem
to Rome. Sharing Good News with all.

Fill us Spirit of God
With energy of your love
Our will is your own

Romans

Paul introduces himself to the Christians in Rome by saying, "Jesus was kind to me and chose me to be an apostle, so that people of all nations would obey and have faith." (Romans 1:5). Paul preached that God's kindness was undeserved, for all have sinned and fallen short of the glory of God.

God desires to save
all who have faith and believe.
No one excluded.

Praise God, revealed
in Jesus kindness and love.
May Jesus be kind to you.

Evil in Book of Roman

Saint Paul spoke of his own soul saying,

Instead of doing
what I know to be right,
I do what is wrong.

(Romans 7:19)

Paul had serious trouble with human sexuality. He strongly condemned women having sex with other women and men having sex with other men (6:26-27). These are personal choices, and religious leaders have no right to make these choices for others. How do we make good decisions? This is the gift of Jesus' gentle life and tender teachings that give us new ideals for the living of our lives in society.

Let love be your guide.
No one who loves will harm others.
Love is what's required.
Romans 13:8-10

Love freely given
and love freely received.
Accept gift given.

Good News of Gospel—
Jesus will be kind to you.
God's gift forever!
Romans 16:20-27

1 and 2 Corinthians

There is a voice that
doesn't use words. Listen. —Rumi

In 1 Corinthians, Paul writes to settle disputes in the church.

His gospel is relational love that heals division. In 2 Corinthians

Paul challenges the followers of Jesus to be generous,
as God is generous to all. An offering is taken to help the suffering
Christians in Jerusalem. He ends the letter by saying,
"I pray that Jesus will be kind to you." (2 Cor. 16:23).

Love is kind and patient—
Not jealous, boastful, or proud.
Love never fails.

God gives to us
gifts of faith, hope, and love.
The greatest is love.

Cross and Resurrection is Central in Paul's Epistles

"Christ died for our sins,
as the Scriptures say,
He was buried,
and three days later
he was raised to life."

1 Corinthians 15:3-4

I walk in nature

Shadow of cross falls on path

Sadness grips my heart

A snowshoe hare squalls

All of Nature is weeping

Lynx with food for kits

Searching for meaning

Stained with bloodshed and travail

Grief of centuries fall

Pain of families

From loss of children in school shooting

Sadness rings in ears

Look up at the sky

Blazing in glory for all

God's light shines

Search for meaning in life
I crave beauty and goodness
Yet haunted by loss

Who told the geese
It was time to take wing and fly
Opening magic vistas

In our search for meaning in life
We crave beauty and goodness
Yet we are haunted by loss
and the terror at the loss of loved ones

The voice that told the geese
It was time to go Speaks to us
Bringing hope of new victories
Winging their way before and above us

Opening magic portals
to a new dimension
of truth and beauty
Goodness and love

Galatians

"I pray that God will be kind to you." —See Galatians 1:1-10
The Greek word, χαρις, is found in the New Testament about
175 times, in 24 of the 27 books; and it is usually translated as
grace. However, the Contemporary English Version of the
American Bible Society almost always translates χαρις as
kindness. My own study of the χαρις word group from its early
Greek origins to the time of the New Testament justifies this
translation as kindness. As used in the covenant between God
and God's people, grace always implies a gracious turning of
God in kindness to heal brokenness. Almost all the Epistles
begin and end with gracious kindness.

> Kindness in our thoughts,
> making them good and loving.
> Leading to justice.
>
> May kindness be in our hands and feet
> so that we may be
> of service to others.
>
> May kindness be in our whole being –
> Making us one with God, one with all people,
> and one with the universe.
>
> I don't know how to define kindness,
> but I know for sure when I feel it.

Kindness is the language
known around the world.

As children of God,
show love for all those who suffer.
Give liberally.

Ephesians

Be kind one to another, tenderhearted, forgiving one another,

even as God has forgiven you. —Ephesians 4:32

Thousands of children

have been separated

from their parents at our borders,

some just infants

in their mother's arms.

And this is still happening.

We are a better nation than this!

A Revolution of Kindness

My loving parents taught me

that kindness is hidden

in every word and deed.

Bible reveals kindness

in the prophets and Psalmists

of Old Testament.

In Jesus' gentle life

and tender teachings empowered by God

in New Testament.

In my ministry,
I saw transforming power
of kind words and deeds.

Contemplative lifestyle
reveals kindness hiding
in all of nature.

Shares with one and all.
Nature is unselfishly kind—
Without distinction.

Let us learn to love,
openly sharing nature,
not possessing it.

Instead of building walls,
let us build bridges
to span our differences.

A kindness revolution calls
for courageous action of all faiths—
Quiet transformations.

We're one with suffering.

Walking caravans of refugees.

Seeking a haven.

Kind world of justice

is struggling to be born.

Be kind to all.

(Ephesians 4:32)

A revolution of kindness is a vision of social justice.

It is about gender sensitive tough love that accepts people

of all nations and all sexual persuasions as precious

children of God with talents to share in ministry.

It is a call for the renewal and rebirth of the church.

Philippians

The Apostle Paul wrote the Epistle of Philippians
from prison, but he writes as one grounded in
the goodness of God and joy in service to others.
Paul is happy because he has experienced kindness by the followers
of Christ in Philippi.

Paul encouraged them to show love for each other,
and serve each other in the spirit of Christ—

> Christ was truly God.
> But he did not try to remain
> equal with God.

> He gave up everything,
> and became a servant when
> He became like us.

Christer was humble.

He obeyed God and even died

on a cross.

Then God gave Christ the highest place

and honored his name above all others.

At the name of Jesus everyone will bow down,

those in heaven, on earth, and under the earth.

And to the glory of God the Father

everyone will openly agree,

Jesus Christ is Lord! (2:6-11).

Paul closes this joyful letter with his favorite prayer—
"I pray that Jesus will be kind to you." (See 4:23).

Colossians

You are God's people

Be gentle, kind, and humble

Jesus is our model

1 and 2 Thessalonians

Faith, Hope, and Love

God loves us and in kindness has given us a wonderful hope—
A hope that encourages us, helps us do what is good, and
always say what is loving. (See, 2 Thessalonians 2:16-17.)
For Paul as he penned these verses, as for Jesus and the
Jewish scriptures, love is the greatest commandment.
Faith in God who first loves us, is the ground on which love is
based. Also, In times of enslavement to fear, It is hope
that keeps faith and love alive and adventurous. Faith in the
goodness of God has been shattered. Love has been
cheapened and has lost its power to transform. It is hope that
springs eternal. Hope keeps the heart beating!

Emily Dickinson wrote—

> "Hope is the thing with feathers
> That perches in the soul,
> And sings the tune without the words,
> And never stops at all."

This first verse of her poem about the birds she loved

so much is one of the most popular of Emily's poems.

Its greatness is that it transforms hope into a songbird

that is ever present in the human soul.

It sings always and when times get tough.

Hope springs eternal and inspires the soul.

This is a good summary of hope's meaning.

It makes one want to fly like a bird.

1 and 2 Timothy

When I want to understand a book, I look carefully
at the introduction and the conclusion for they frame
the message. Paul starts and ends his message to Timothy
by stating, I am an apostle of Jesus and I pray that God and
Jesus will be kind to all of you.
(2 Timothy 1:2; 4:23).

Timothy had a special relationship with Paul.
He was like a faithful son to Paul,
and Paul refers to him in five of his letters.

Timothy was sent by Paul to the new churches
as Paul's trouble shooter,
often to restore controversy and bring peace.

I pray that God will
be kind and merciful to you.
Bless you with peace.

Θεοπνευστος

The Greek word, Θεοπνευστος, is found in the New Testament only in 2 Timothy 3:16. And here it is used to describe γραφή. The verse is best translated as "All scripture divinely inspired is useful for teaching." It does not say, "All scripture is divinely inspired." The English verb "is" that is found in most translations of the verse—

Should not be seen as
equating divine inspiration
with all scripture.

Karl Bart wrote often, "The Bible contains the word of God." And this is different from saying "The Bible is the word of God."

I think this is a wise distinction. The Bible is a very diverse collection of writings that reflects different cultural views and world views. It would be a serious mistake to let this one word from one Epistle shape our whole view of the Bible and its meaning for the Church today.

As a linguist who studied Hebrew and Greek and translated most of the New Testament from Greek into English in my Ph. D. studies in New Testament, I humbly suggest that the biblical teaching of kindness is the best hermeneutic.

It is the best prism through which to interpret all the Bible.

(See my book, A Relational Hermeneutic of Kindness).

Ministry can be summed up in this faith statement:

God meets each occasion of life with kindness and lures all

through loving kindness to become their very best self. The

Kindness show to oneself, family, and to all persons is

the most healing and transforming force in the world.

I pray that God will

be kind and merciful to you.

Bless you with peace.

(See 1 Timothy 1:1-2 and 2 Timothy:1-2)

Be faithful and loving.

Be dependable and gentle.

God will be kind to you.

Titus

In our world where radical evil is rampant

and fear driven violence is increasing,

here is a key faith question that needs our best thought:

Is there any reality working for good that calls us

to give our whole heart, soul, and mind with total commitment?

Yes, God is with us and for us! Our most urgent need is to

cooperate with God's loving purpose. Living God's kindness will

save us and our world from violence.

God is merciful
God is good and kind
God blesses us with peace
(See Titus 1:4 and 3:4-5).

Philemon

Philemon is about the transforming power of the

Gospel: Tender Christian love that changes lives

and relationships, regardless of class standing

or any other condition. The letter is so short

that it is not even divided by chapters.

Like many of the New Testament Epistles,

Philemon begins and ends with the message of kindness.

(Verses 3 and 25).

"I pray

that the Lord Jesus Christ

will be kind to you." (Verse 25).

Hebrews

Hebrews was written to show the uniqueness of Jesus for Christian faith. Jesus is presented as the Son of God, greater than Moses and Joshua.

Jesus understands our weakness.
He overcame his own temptations.
With kindness Jesus helps us.

(Hebrews 4:16)

Faith makes us sure
Of what we can not see
Faith pleases God

(Hebrews 11)

James

James is addressed to Christians scattered through out the Roman Empire. Even though James is written as a letter, it appears to be more like a small book filled with instructions for daily living. One of the central beliefs is that faith is demonstrated by actions. Thus, the Book of James offers encouragement for faithful actions.

Faith is demonstrated

By being patient and kind

Doing good deeds

Faith means

Patient, humble, kind actions

Growing strong in prayer

(James 5:7-20)

1 and 2 Peter

The Epistles of Peter were written in a time of suffering
to offer encouragement and hope. Peter reminds them of
Jesus's suffering. He uses poetic imagery to inspire hope.

1 Peter begins with a prayer—

That God will be kind to you
and will keep on giving you peace. (1 Peter 1:2, 2 Peter 1:2).

"Humans wither like grass,
and their glory fades
like wild flowers.

Grass dries up,
and flowers fall to the ground.
God stands forever." (1:24).

"Christ died once for our sins,
an innocent person died
for those who are guilty.
Christ did this
to bring you to God.
When his body was put to death,
and his spirit was made alive. (1 Peter 3:18).

2 Peter ends with this challenge—

"Let the kindness
from our Savior Jesus Christ
help you keep growing." (3:18).

1, 2, and 3 John

"Love overcomes fear." —1 John 4:18

"The teleology of the Universe is directed to the production of Beauty." Alfred North Whitehead, *Adventure of Ideas, p. 265.*

Fear knocks at the door
faithful love lifts the latch
fear is not there

Be tender
as a mother's nursing heart.
Gentleness flows.

Nature's grace
gives rise to a Higher Love
Amazing Grace

Universe flows
toward Beauty
Nature's love

Love from heaven above
flows into our heart
Never to Part

The Shape of Love
(I John 4:7)


```
We
must              love          when      other   We become
love          comes from     we     each      God's
each other        God                   love           children.
```

Jude

Jude, the next to last book of the New Testament,
is concerned about defending the followers of Jesus
from false teachings. It begins with a prayer in verse two:

I pray that God will

greatly bless you with kindness.

Live in peace, and love.

Jude closes this short letter with a prayer for God to keep
them free from sin, while joyfully serving God.

Show kindness to all.
Stay free from evil teachings.
Live joyfully.

Revelation

Revelation begins with these words—

"I pray that you will be blessed with kindness and peace from God, who is and was, and is coming. May you receive kindness and peace . . . before the throne of God." (1:4).

Revelation closes the New Testament with the prayer,

"May Jesus be kind to all of you." (22:21).

In poetic language
This is how I understand
John's message—

Hello God,
A vision came to me.
This is what I saw.
People suffering.
Praying, how long, God.
Kindness is your hope.

Words were spoken.
Inspiring songs were sung.
Jesus will be kind to you.

John's vision—
A new heaven and new earth.
Comes by kindness and peace.

This evil age will pass,
God will create a new world—
Heaven on earth.

The human psyche
is both good and evil.
God is totally good.

Hell put to flight.
Illness eradicated.
Kindness wins the day.

You will be blessed
with kindness and peace from God.
Jesus loves you.

Lord Jesus come.
Be kind to everyone.
world without end.

Alaska Adventures in Kindness (2011-present)

Kindness is like a beautiful
stained glass window
that gathers the light of heaven
and warms all in its glow

Our move to Alaska to help with our grandchildren was going home.

It was a movement for me into nature, reminiscence of childhood on

the family farm. It was also a more contemplative lifestyle shaped by

the beauty of Alaska. I had met Thomas Merton, a monk at

Gethsemane Monastery when I was a seminary student in Kentucky.

I had gotten all his books and especially liked his poetry and

contemplative life-style. I discovered that Merton took a trip to Alaska

and explored building a hermitage there to be more isolated.

In moving to Alaska, I felt I was fulfilling his cherished desire.

When contemplating, I see a Nurturing God of love, patiently,

giving value to all things. Inviting and empowering us to join

in this adventure. Persons nurtured in nature are compassionate,

empathetic, and always caring for others.

(See Kathleen Witkowska Tarr, We Are All Poets Here, for
Thomas Merton's 1968 journey to Alaska. This book is an excellent
story about spiritual seeking).

Gift of Family

When a lot of change is in the air
I find inspiration, comfort, and hope
In each new Alpenglow sunrise.

With loving family
The sun is always rising
Showing us the way

Solace of Solitary Places

Nation polarized

Seek solace of solitary places

Find that God is good

Rest in

kindness

and peace

The kindness and love

we show to our world family

is a healing force

(Based on Revelation 1:4-5)

Rainbows

Rainbow bright colors
Rubies and emeralds
 Transforms mountains

—See Revelation 4:3

In step with God's love
as you wait for Jesus to show
how kind God is.

—Jude 1:21

I pray that Jesus
    will be kind
    to all of you.

—Revelation 22:21

My poetry book,
Poet of the Universe: A Vision of Beauty and Goodness,
speaks from unknown realms

.

Poems inspire
beauty, wonder, and hope
in our daily lives.

I do not write my poetry
I walk in Alaska's beauty
Nature whispers secrets

I listen carefully
Nature is the real poet
I am the pencil

156

Love Tango

Mother and calf dancing

a tango of tenderness.

Dance with great joy.

(For other moose photos and nature poems see my book,
BEARS AND MOOSE OF ALASKA: Nature Poetry.)

Conclusion

A poetic journey takes us back to birth and childhood.

To parents/caregivers who nurtured us in family love

and great joy. One's journey seen as a poetic spiritual memoir,

shaped in the telling and retelling of biblical stories,

is filled with both faith and doubt, earthly sorrows and

heavenly sunlight.

(See my book, Down on the Farm in Georgia: A Poetic Memoir.)

This poetic journey through the Bible has focused on God

calling all who will respond to communicate God's love aims

and purposes for all people, in an ever widening circle. A one

sentence summary might be: God calls through the

needs of others. Many of the poems have expressed

this idea. Purity of heart is revealed in how one treats others.

In these poems I have suggested God has concern for all

people. If God is the God of all people, then religious bodies

must discover ways and means to address the

critical needs of an oppressed humanity. How well are we

fulfilling this challenge? The call of Jesus is still,
"You must deny self, take up your cross, and follow me."
God's story is much larger than the biblical story
of judges, prophets, and apostles. God's story is larger
than the one thousand year written history recorded
in the Bible. God's story did not begin with Genesis or end with
the last book of the Bible. Writing these sacred poems on
the Bible is a continuation of God's story and the faith story
of the people of God. God's mysterious story is always moving
forward and upward in time and space. One stellar sentence in
Rev. 1:4, the last book of the Bible, captures this spirit: "I pray
you will be blessed with kindness and peace from God, who is,
and was, and is coming."

Every day new poems are written in God's adventurous story.
God is the poet of the universe, in tender patience leading.
In sharing these faith poems, I have sought to join God
in this zestful adventurous mystery filled journey.
The awe-inspiring mystery of God draws us onward and upward.
The authoritative reality is not how we have
shaped the poems, but how the Bible's poems have shaped us,
as memory becomes a flame lighting our path. May these faith
stories continue to break down racial and gender barriers that
separate us. and may they unite us as one in the family of God.

Gentle teachings of religious leaders that inspired these poems

help me to be a more loving husband, father, grandfather,

neighbor, teacher, and Minister of word and sacrament.

I pass the poems on to you with the prayer that you will

translate them in ever new and exciting ways so that this

process of going forward and upward will never end. As a poet,

I am aware of the great chasm between vision and fulfillment.

Yet, we must press on, for—

The adventure
belongs to
the adventurous!

Let your Kindness shine brightly on us.
(Psalm 3:6)

D. Cole

Psalms 46:10, "Calm down and learn that I am God," is a key verse for seeing, hearing, and living the Bible as a poetic journey.

The quieter you are
The more you can see and hear
Be still and know God
Solitude in the beauty of nature
Nurtures calmness of our soul

A World Vision

Sit among flowers.

Touch tassels of Jesus' robe.

Feel God's love and care.

Sit among flowers.

Touch Mother Teresa's robe.

Care for poor children.

Sit among flowers.

Touch the Buddha's simple robe.

Teach kindness for all.

Purity of heart

is revealed in how well

one treats others.

Nature is rebirth

Always renewing beauty

Nature is the poet.

A walk in nature

is a walk in eternity—

A walk in wonder!

Life is nature's novel.

Let the mother moose write it.

Family felicity!

To know and to live
the Bible as poetry—
A worthy pursuit!

Messenger from God
Wrapped in soft angel wings
Sing heavenly songs

Loved ones rejoicing
Dancing around sparkling throne
Eternity is now

There is no death
for one who is loved,
love is eternal.

Going Forward

*Our greatest glory is not in never falling, but in rising
every time we fall.*—Confucius

Most societies developed mythic stories of how the world began
and how humans came into existence. Those stories have varied in
purpose and meaning. As they were told and retold they changed
and grew. Once the biblical stories were written down, canonized,
and given ultimate authority for daily living, they lost some of their
magic that transforms. (See my book, The Story of the Bible:
Authority, Inspiration, Canonization, and Translation).

A journey through the Bible demonstrates how the people of God
changed and reshaped their faith stories to meet current needs
in the changing communities. What shape will these faith stories
take in the future? How will the world-wide COVID epidemic end,
and how will this experience shape our understanding of God
and the Bible?

Breaking News—

god has COVID-19
variants from alpha to omega
world breathed on god

world was unvaccinated
did not even wear a mask
god has become ill

god has COVID-19
god is on ventilator
in intensive care

god can't hear our prayers
the church bells are not ringing
god can't meet our needs

Jesus crucified.
Darkness fell upon the earth.
Wrapped in grave clothes.

Placed in a tomb
Stone rolled against entrance
Mary comes to tomb

Easter morning
Stone is rolled away
Jesus is alive!

Breaking Good News!
God has survived death before.
Jesus is alive!

One of the needs in biblical studies today is to baptize the Bible in the science of genetic research. Wisdom of God comes not in never falling, but rising when we fall. Science will show us how to rise. The book, THE CODE BREAKER by Walter Isaacson, featuring Jennifer Doudna, shows how gene editing is writing a new story of the past, present, and future life. Nature and nature's God is seen with new eyes. God, the Poet of the world, is changing as our world changes.

"Let the beauty we love be what we do. There are hundreds of ways to kneel and kiss the ground." —Rumi

Pansies/violets
have such lovely faces
Beauty in all faces

I bring a flower

The sweetest one I could find

Love blossom kisses

The Bible: A Poetic Journey, on the deepest level is a poetic memoir. It is a never ending journey. Beth, my wife, asked, how long have you worked on this book. My answer was, since I was a twinkle in my parents eyes, an embryo in my mother's womb. It is a journey without end. The book has been written and erased many times. I feel that God who is described in one stellar sentence in Revelation 1:8, as "I am the Alpha and Omega, the one who is, and was, and is coming," is with me and inspiring me with hope.

A Challenge for Going Forward

God is in the world and for the world, in us and for us, tenderly saving all that can be saved. This relational conception of God has implications for how we live our lives in relationship with all people in ever-widening circles of faith. With code-breaking research in genetics being done around the world, we are gaining new insights into gender. What it means to be male and female is changing.

This book has shown that the seeds for this new understanding were planted throughout the Bible.

In the Jewish patriarchal society that dominated the writing of the Old Testament, God was basically presented as male. Yet, even the Old Testament writers presented breaking news—

Hosea described God in chapter 11
as a Mother caring for her child.

I loved you as a child
I fed you at my breast
I taught you to walk

In Hosea's imagery—

God is TRANS
Changes from male to female,
from father to mother.

Hosea was a big influence on Jesus' tender teachings. And this passage alone opens the door to applying new code-breaking genetic research to our understanding of the Bible. As Matthew's account of the gentle Galilean ministry of Jesus comes to an end, he has this news bulletin—Breaking News: Matthew 23:37-39—

God has transitioned
Becoming a mother hen
Gathering her chicks

With these breaking news passages in the Old and New Testaments, the Church can no longer use the Bible as a weapon to bash LGBTQ+ individuals, and deny them the right to Christian ministry. In the Bible, God is TRANS. TRANS is good.

There comes a time for every poet, when you lay your pencil and poem down and say, for now it is finished. My students, or someone reading this book, can take it up and continue the biblical faith journey. I will continue to add to the message as I daily experience, The Bible: A Poetic Journey, in my daily worship and service.

Life's always changing
Stars in the sky live and die
Star dust in our soul
Rise up and shine like the sun
Sparkle like the Milky Way

Appendix A, Ten Key Bible Verses on Kindness

1. "God's love and **kindness** will shine upon us like the sun that rises in the sky. On us who live in the dark shadow of death, this light will shine to guide us into a life of peace" (Luke 1:78-79).

> God's loving kindness
> shines as bright as the sun
> with the gift of peace

2. Jesus said, "Come to me, all of you who are tired from carrying heavy loads, and I will give your rest. Take my yoke and put it on you, and learn from me, because I am **gentle and humble in spirit**; and you will find rest. For the yoke I will give you is easy and the load I will put on you is light." (Matthew 11:28-30).

> Learn from Jesus
> Gentle and humble teacher
> Gives the gift of peace

3. Jesus said, "**Blessed are the gentle**, they will receive what God has promised!" (Matthew 5:5).

> Jesus promises
> Blessed are the gentle
> God's gift to all

4. Paul in imitating the spirit of Jesus, grounds kindness in the being of God, "You are God's people so **be gentle, kind, humble, and meek**." (Colossians 3:12).

You are God's family
Be gentle, kind, and humble
Jesus is our model

5. **"Be kind and merciful**, and forgive others, just as God forgave you because of Jesus." (Ephesians 4:32).

Forgive all others
Just as God forgives you
Merciful kindness

6. Jesus taught, "People who are well do not need a doctor, but only those who are sick. Go and find out what is meant by the scripture that says, 'It is **kindness** that I want, not animal sacrifices.' I have not come to call respectable people, but outcasts." (Matthew 9:12-13).

God, friend of outcasts
Healer of those who are hurting
kindness medicine

7. "I pray that you will **be blessed with kindness** and peace from God, who is and was and is coming. May you receive kindness and peace from Jesus, the faithful witness." (Revelation 1:4-5).

God came in Jesus
To bless with kindness and peace
Go share the good news

8. "A man with leprosy came to Jesus and knelt down. **Jesus felt sorry for him** so he put his hands on him and said, 'You are well.'" (Mark 1:40-41).

Leper came to Jesus
Jesus touches untouchable
Healing compassion

9. "Jesus said, "Don't worry about your life. **God will take care of you.**" (Luke 12:22-26).

Good news of Jesus
Don't worry about your life
God takes care of you

10. "I pray that **Jesus will be kind to all of you.**" (Revelation 22:21).

Bible summary
Jesus is kind to everyone
Journey in kindness

Appendix B, Jesus' Words of Kindness

Πραυς, Πραυτης (gentle, gentleness)

In reference to persons, πραυς and πραυτης, the noun and adjective form, are best translated as gentle and gentleness. The two terms are used about 15 times in the Greek New Testament and may also be translated as meek, humble, friendly, or pleasant, in both adjective and noun forms.

In the Old Testament gentleness is rooted in God. The inheritance of the land promised to Abraham and his descendants comes to the gentle who wait---"The humble will possess the land and enjoy prosperity and peace" (See Psalms 37:9-11).

In the New Testament, the mission of Jesus is the fulfillment of gentleness. In fact, it is the self-designation of Jesus in Matthew 11:28-30--"Come to me, all of you who are tired from carrying heavy loads, and I will give your rest. Take my yoke and put it on you, and learn from me, because I am gentle and humble in spirit; and you will find rest. For the yoke I will give you is easy and the load I will put on you is light."

That Jesus was πραυς, tender of heart, is also supported by the Letters of Paul in the New Testament and in non-biblical sources like the Gospel of Thomas, the Sibylline Oracles, and Pistis Sophia. In Second Corinthians chapter ten, verse one, Paul wrote, "Jesus himself was humble and gentle." Colossians 3:12 grounds kindness in the being of God, "You are God's people so be gentle, kind, humble, and meek." Titus 3:4 also describes God as kind.

ταπεινος, ταπεινοω, ταπεινωσις

This group of Greek words occurs thirty-four times in the New Testament, and they are usually translated "lowly", but they carry the connotation of gentle or gentleness..
χρηστος

Jesus used χρηστος twice, once to describe the nature of God as kind to the ungrateful and wicked (Luke 6:35) and once as a selfdesignation, describing himself as one who is kind or merciful in what he requires of those who come to him (Matthew 11:30).

Paul understood kindness in this way as well. In Romans 2:4 he writes about the "fullness of the χρηστητος, kindness, of God and God's patience, μακροθυμιας. In Romans 11:22 Paul speaks of the kindness of God being shown for the ones who have fallen away from God. In these uses of kindness Paul is true to the Old Testament understanding of the gracious action of God and he sees this fulfilled in the actions of Jesus. In Galatians 5:22-23 Paul listed kindness as one of the fruits of the Spirit that should be growing in the life of Christians.

1 Peter 2:2-3, shows the saving action of kindness. "Like new born infants, long for the pure spiritual milk , so that by it you may grow into salvation. If indeed you have tasted that the Lord is good and kind, χρηστος.

The crowing verse on kindness in the New Testament for Christians is Ephesians 4:32---"Be kind and merciful, and forgive others, just as God forgave you because of Christ." This key verse links kindness with forgiveness and anchors these qualities in God's own actions with the gentle ministry of Jesus.

ελεος

Ελεος occurs three times in Matthew and is usually translated as mercy. The Good News Bible translates it as kindness, its original Old Testament meaning. This can be seen in Matthew 9:9-11, which reports Jesus' call of Matthew to discipleship. After Jesus called Matthew, he was having a meal in Matthew's house with other tax collectors and outcasts. Some Pharisees saw this and asked, Jesus' disciples, "Why does Jesus eat with such people?" Jesus heard them and answered, "People who are well do not need a doctor, but only those who are sick. Go and find out what is meant by the scripture that says, 'It is kindness that I want, not animal sacrifices.' I have not come to call respectable people, but outcasts." This and the other two passages in Matthew that use ελεος (12:7; 23:23) characterize Jesus' ministry as merciful kindness toward the outcasts and demand the same for the disciples who would follow Jesus.

Ελεος, mercy, occurs six times in Luke. Five of these are in the birth announcements of John and Jesus and refer to the wonderful kindness and tender mercy God is showing toward the people of God (Luke 1:50, 54, 58, 72, 78). Tender mercy is most relevant to the theme of "Gentle Galilean Glories:" "Our God is merciful and tender. God will cause the bright dawn of salvation to rise on us and to shine from heaven on all those who live in the dark shadow of death, to guide our path to peace."

σπλαγχνον, σπλανγχνιζομαι

In Luke 1:78, ελεος is combined with σπλαγχνον and is translated as "tender mercy." The verb form, σπλαγχνιζομαι, occurs twelve times in Matthew, Mark, and Luke, the Synoptic Gospels, and is usually translated as "having compassion." Ten of these represent Jesus as one in whom divine compassion is present. Jesus is moved with compassion toward a man with a dreaded skin disease (Mark 1:41). the crowd of people who were like sheep without a shepherd (Mark 6:34; Matthew 14:14), and the hungry crowd (Mark 8:2: Matthew 15:32).

Jesus also had compassion on the widow of Nain and raised her dead son back to life (Luke 7:11-17), and with compassion he restored sight to two blind men (Matthew 20:29-34). The verb, having compassion, also had a central place in three of Jesus' most significant parables: the unforgiving servant who had been forgiven with compassion (Matthew 18:21-33), the good Samaritan whose heart was filled with compassion when he saw the wounded man lying by the roadside (Luke 10:25-37. The whole Samaritan story is summarized as an act of kindness. and the parable of the prodigal son, better called the waiting father, for it is the father who saw the son a long way off and had compassion and ran to meet him (Luke 15:11-32, especially see verse 20).

In all of these teachings of Jesus that use σπλάγχνον and σπλαγχνιζομαι, Jesus' human emotions are described in the strongest terms possible in order to stress the tender compassion with which God claims persons in saving grace. This was also true of all the other Greek words we have studied.

Χαρις

The χαρις word group appears about 175 times in the New Testament, with the majority occurring in the Epistles of Paul. Most English versions of the Bible translate χαρις as grace or gracious. However, the Contemporary English Version of the American Bible Society almost always translates χαρις as kindness. A survey of the history of the term from its early Greek origins to the time of the New Testament justifies this use of kindness. In both the Old Testament and the New Testament the Hebrew and Greek words usually translated as grace imply a kind turning of one person to another in an act of assistance. God's covenant grace also implies kindness.

Perhaps the most significant uses of χαρις come in the Book of Revelation. At a time when the followers of Jesus are being persecuted and dying for their faith, John the writer of Revelation holds up a vision of the kind Jesus. The book starts with this prayer: "I pray that you will be blessed with kindness and peace from God, who is and was and is coming. May you receive kindness and peace from Jesus, the faithful witness" (Based on Revelation 1:4-5 from the Greek New Testament). Revelation ends with this prayer: "I pray that Jesus will come soon and be kind to all of you" (Based on Revelation 22:20-21 from the Greek New Testament. For a fuller treatment of this Greek word see my book, *The Book of Revelation: Jesus' Kindness Transforms Suffering*).

The word clusters we have examined leave no room for doubt that Jesus was gentle, lowly, and kind. What struck me as I studied Jesus' language of kindness was how Jesus described himself as being gentle. Thus, we are on solid ground when we speak of Jesus as kindness. The kindness of God shines in the words and deeds of Jesus. The disciples and the crowds who followed Jesus saw the glory of God shining through his gentle Galilean glories. Can there be any doubt that Jesus lived and taught kindness? The rich cluster of words described above make kindness a good choice for our presenting the Bible as a poetic journey in tenderness.

Breaking News: John 1:1-18

We saw God's glory
God's kindness came into the world
Showing God is love

Tender teachings of Jesus
clothed in science and the humanities
are our visionary road map.

The list of my books on the next page were all born from
my masters thesis, HERMENEUTICAL THEORY IN
TRANSITION AS REFLECTED IN INTERPRETATION: A
JOURNAL OF BIBLE AND THEOLOGY (1947-1966); and my
doctoral dissertation, BAPTISM AND THE LORD'S SUPPER IN
THE GOSPEL OF JOHN: A HERMENEUTICAL INQUIRY.
This parentage is especially true of my book, A Relational
Hermeneutic of Kindness. On the deepest level, all of my 50 year
preaching ministry, published articles, Sunday School lessons, and
devotions were born from this parentage and nurtured in God's
relational kindness. My poetry books for the last decade have
especially sought to unite science and the humanities in one clear
voice that brings healing and transformation. Relational theology
sees God in the world and for the world, in us and for us. In this
relational kindness people of all sexualities, gender identities and
expressions are equally loved by God and are an integral part of
God's diverse family. God calls all persons, and all who respond
become coworkers with God's novel aims and purposes.

Poetic journey
into myth offers guidance
In time of pandemic

Myth wrapped in kindness
liberates our culture from bondage
to individualism

OTHER BOOKS BY DWAYNE COLE

A Center that Holds: Adventures in Kindness
Alpenglow Miracles: Fire Dance of Wonder
A Prayer of Blessing: As You Go Remember This
A Relational Hermeneutic of Kindness
A Relational Trinity of Kindness
BEARS AND MOOSE OF ALASKA: Nature Poetry
Clouds of Inspiration
Down on the Farm in Georgia: A Poetic Memoir
Dragonfly Magic
Gentle Galilean Glories: The Tender Teachings of Jesus
God and Evil: An Ode to Kindness
Jesus' Transforming Beatitudes: Selected Sermons from Year A
Jesus' Transforming Love: Selected Sermons from Year B
Jesus' Transforming Gentle Teachings: Selected Sermons from Year C
Kindness Is Every Step
Lone Leaf Dancing
Poems Inspired by Process Philosophy
Poet of the Universe: A Vision of Beauty and Goodness
The Apostles' Creed: A Living Creed for the Living Church
The Book of Revelation: Jesus' Kindness Transforms Suffering
The Serenity Prayer: A Pathway to Peace and Happiness
The Story of the Bible: Authority, Inspiration, Canonization, and
Translation
TREES AND DRIFTWOOD: Poetic Ecology
WINGS OF INSPIRATION

Parson's Porch Books

The Bible: A Poetic Journey
ISBN: Softcover
Copyright © 2022 by Dwayne Cole

Parson's Porch Books is an imprint of Parson's Porch *&* Company (PP*&*C) in Cleveland, Tennessee. PP*&*C is an innovative organization which raises money by publishing books of noted authors, representing all genres. Its face and voice is **David Russell Tullock** (dtullock@parsonsporch.com).

Parson's Porch *&* Company *turns books into bread & milk* by sharing its profits with the poor.

www.parsonsporch.com

www.ingramcontent.com/pod-product-compliance
Lightning Source LLC
Chambersburg PA
CBHW051520120626

46551CB00012B/1008